Building Teams

SpiritBuilt Leadership 8

Malcolm Webber

Published by:

Strategic Press
Division of Strategic Global Assistance, Inc.

513 South Main St., Suite 2
Elkhart, IN 46516
U.S.A.
Toll free: 1-844-532-3371
www.sgai.org

Our secure online bookstore:
www.StrategicPress.org

Copyright © Malcolm Webber, 2001

ISBN: 9781888810240

All Scripture references are from the New International Version of the Bible, unless otherwise noted.

Printed in the United States of America

Table of Contents

Introduction 5

1. The Biblical Basis of Teams 7
2. Working Groups 13
3. The Nature of Teams 19
4. The Benefits of Teams 35
5. The Characteristics of a Healthy Team 39

Introduction

The most effective churches and ministries today are the ones that work hard at developing teams.

There are different kinds of teams we can use. There are long-term teams, such as leadership teams, and short-term teams that are brought together to accomplish specific purposes.

The concept of teams is not new. Since creation, men have formed groups of various kinds to accomplish various purposes. We are born into groups (families), we are educated in groups (classes), we play sports in groups (sports teams), we work in groups (companies), we fight in groups (armies), and we worship and serve God in groups (churches).

We spend most of our waking lives in groups of some kind, yet there are fewer areas of living in which we are less successful than that of living and working together. Man's inability to live and work in harmony confronts us on every side: between nations we have wars, in families we have divorces, between companies we have bitter competition, within churches we have strife and division.

It is considerably easier to work individually. Yet there is great power released when we work as a team. Additionally, God's design is for teams.

Most of what we say here applies in the context of *leadership teams* in churches and Christian ministries, although the principles will mostly apply to any kind of team at any level.

Malcolm Webber, Ph.D.
Strategic Press, Elkhart, Indiana
2001

Before You Begin

Please read the following statements. If you think the statement is true, circle the T next to the item number. If you think the statement is false, circle the F next to the item number *and* explain why you think the statement is false:

T   F   1.   The idea of working in teams is a popular and practical concept, but it has no biblical basis.

T   F   2.   Any group of people working together is a team.

T   F   3.   In effective teams, every member contributes during team meetings.

T   F   4.   Before giving a team member negative criticism, it is wise to first state something positive the person has done.

T   F   5.   To maintain respect, a team leader should remain aloof from team members.

chapter 1

The Biblical Basis of Teams

Before we examine specific issues regarding teams, we must first establish their biblical basis.

1. The triune nature of God.

    God is three and yet God is one. The eternal nature of God provides a wonderful picture of the perfect team.

    a. Each member of the Godhead is equal.

        Jesus and the Father are equal:

        I and the Father are one. (John 10:30)

        Jesus and the Holy Spirit are equal:

        And I will ask the Father, and He will give you another Counselor to be with you forever – the Spirit of truth… I will not leave you as orphans; I will come to you. (John 14:16-18)

        Father, Son and Holy Spirit are equal.

        … baptizing them in the name of the Father and of the Son and of the Holy Spirit, (Matt. 28:19)

        May the grace of the Lord Jesus Christ, and the love of God, and the fellowship of the Holy Spirit be with you all. (2 Cor. 13:14)

There is one body and one Spirit – just as you were called to one hope when you were called – one Lord, one faith, one baptism; one God and Father of all, who is over all and through all and in all. (Eph. 4:4-6)

b. Yet there are clear distinctions of responsibility and function within the Godhead:

… who have been chosen according to the foreknowledge of God the Father, through the sanctifying work of the Spirit, for obedience to Jesus Christ and sprinkling by His blood … (1 Pet. 1:2)

According to Peter, these are the distinct roles of the members of the Godhead: the Father elected us (origin of salvation), the Son came and died for us (means of salvation), and now the Holy Spirit applies both our election and salvation through His power in conversion (effecting of salvation). Thus, the entire triune Godhead is involved in salvation: the Father chooses, the Son atones, and the Spirit applies.

c. The Godhead always acts as One in perfect unity:

Then God said, "Let Us make man in Our image, in Our likeness …" (Gen. 1:26)

Come, let Us go down and confuse their language so they will not understand each other. (Gen. 11:7)

Then I heard the voice of the Lord saying, "Whom shall I send? And who will go for Us?"… (Is. 6:8)

> *There are different kinds of gifts, but the same Spirit. There are different kinds of service, but the same Lord. There are different kinds of working, but the same God works all of them in all men. (1 Cor. 12:4-6)*

This is the eternal nature of God. God has always been triune. God has always existed and acted in community.

2. The creation of man as male and female.

    > *So God created man in His own image, in the image of God He created him; male and female He created them. (Gen. 1:27)*

    Man was created in the image of the triune God. God created man as male and female. Husband and wife are, ideally, to live and work together as a team.

    a. Again we see equality in this relationship:

        > *There is neither Jew nor Greek, slave nor free, male nor female, for you are all one in Christ Jesus. (Gal. 3:28)*

    b. We also see diversity of responsibility and function:

        > *... heirs together of the grace of life ... (1 Pet. 3:7)*

    c. Husband and wife are also intended to live and act together in unity:

        > *"For this reason a man will leave his father and mother and be united to his wife, and the two will become one flesh." (Eph. 5:31)*

3. Jesus and His disciples.

   Jesus did not merely train a group of individuals to be independent spiritual giants. When He sent them out it was in pairs (Mark 6:7), and His ultimate life's purpose – along with dying on the Cross – was to build a team of men to whom He would turn over responsibility for the birthing and leading of His Church.

4. The Body of Christ.

   In 1 Corinthians 12, Paul shares a very clear vision for team ministry within the Church. Here are some of the principles he mentions:

   a. Team members bring different abilities and gifts into the team, and they may all serve in different ways. Yet they all serve in unity to fulfill the same ultimate divine purpose (12:4-6).
   b. The team is made up of many parts (12:7-11) and yet is meant to function in unity (12:12) as Christ unites us and His Spirit empowers us (12:13).
   c. There is no place for an independent spirit if effective team ministry is to occur (12:14-16).
   d. No one member is capable of fulfilling the responsibilities of the whole team (12:17).
   e. God is the One who is strategically building His team, giving each member mutually complementary gifts (12:18-20).
   f. Each member of the team must realize his need for all other members (12:21).
   g. It is often the unseen team members – those who faithfully fulfill their responsibilities whether they are recognized or not – who will be the most honored by God (12:22-24).
   h. In an effective team each member must be concerned not only for his own role but also for the other members of the

team (12:25).

i. We are inextricably linked together (12:26). Consequently, one missing or malfunctioning team member causes the whole team to suffer and lose its effectiveness.

j. We must be committed to one another: to form and participate in effective teams (12:27).

k. God is the One who raises up the team and establishes its order as it pleases Himself (12:28).

l. We should find and fulfill our own special calling in the team – for which God has gifted and prepared us – and not try to do what seems to be the most important (12:29-30).

m. We should earnestly desire to be used in the greatest way possible in the context of the team (12:31a)

n. The team will be most effective when it exists and functions in a relational community of love (12:31b – 13:13).

chapter 2

Working Groups

Just because there is a group of people working together does not make them a "team." Many groups think they are a team when, in reality, they are only a "working group."

Working groups are collection of individuals whose energies are all directed towards their individual roles and responsibilities.

- They make little attempt at living in community.
- Group members are not deeply committed to each other's personal growth and fruitfulness.
- There is little working together. What interaction group members have is primarily to share information or to make decisions to help each individual perform better within his own particular area of responsibility.
- Group members are committed to their own individual agendas without having any overarching, common team-purpose or shared team-vision.
- There is little mutual accountability.

Such working groups may be called "teams" but they are actually only pseudo-teams. They may have an appearance of "teamwork" but there is no real *synergy*. Synergy, in engineering, relates to the manufacturing of products with a mixture of metals of different qualities. When these metals are rightly combined, the resulting new metal (e.g., brass) possesses a strength that its constituents (copper and zinc) did not possess by themselves.

In a working group, while the potential for great things exists due to the individual abilities and skills of the members, yet this potential is never realized due to the way they interrelate. The power of a real team is never released.

A working group of people becomes a team when the whole is greater than the sum of its parts.

The following table lists some of the key differences between working groups and teams:

Differences Between Working Groups and Teams	
Working Groups	**Teams**
Leader-centered	Member-centered
Individual accountability to the leader	Mutual accountability to each other
Vision, goals and working approach set by others	Vision, goals and working approach set by team
Individual agendas	Team agenda
Entirely separate lives	Live and work in community
Organized meetings, delegation	Mutual feedback, open-ended discussion, active problem-solving

Before proceeding to our examination of the nature of teams, please take a moment and complete the following exercise.

EXERCISE

PART 1

Think about a group to which you currently belong. Answer the questions below as they pertain to the functioning of your group.

1 means you strongly disagree. 5 means you strongly agree.

1. Groups meetings are held regularly and everyone attends.
   1   2   3   4   5

2. We talk about and share the same vision and goals for our work.
   1   2   3   4   5

3. We spend most of our meeting time discussing "business," but discussions are open-ended and active.
   1   2   3   4   5

4. We talk through any conflicts and disagreements until they are resolved.
   1   2   3   4   5

5. Group members listen carefully to one another.
   1   2   3   4   5

6. We really trust each other, speaking personally about what we really feel.
   1   2   3   4   5

7. We encourage each other to be creative and to take initiative.
   1   2   3   4   5

8. Each member looks for ways to contribute to the success of other members.
       1   2   3   4   5

9. I am really satisfied being a part of this group.
       1   2   3   4   5

10. We freely give each other credit for jobs well done.
        1   2   3   4   5

11. Group members give and receive feedback to help the group do better.
        1   2   3   4   5

12. We hold each other accountable; each member is accountable to the group.
        1   2   3   4   5

13. Group members really like and respect each other.
        1   2   3   4   5

Total Score _____

PART 2

Reread the questions, this time placing a check mark by each one for which you consciously contributed to improving the group dynamic. Give yourself one point for each check mark.

Total Score _____

SCORING AND INTERPRETATION

For Part 1, if you scored 52 or greater, your group is experiencing authentic team life. Congratulations! If you scored between 39 and 51, there is a positive team identity that can be developed even further. If you scored between 26 and 38, team identity is weak and probably not very satisfying. If you scored below 26, you do not have a team; you are a loose collection of individuals.

For Part 2, if you scored 3 or fewer, you are not taking a strong leadership role in building team identity. If you scored 6 or higher, you are playing a significant role in building your team.

Teams don't just happen; they take a lot of work. Please reflect on what you personally can do to make your group more like a real team:

_____

_____

_____

_____

_____

_____

_____

chapter 3
The Nature of Teams

A team is a small group of people who live and function in loving community, who are deeply committed to each other's personal growth and success, who possess complementary gifts and skills, who are committed to a common vision, specific goals, and approach, and for which commitment they hold each other mutually accountable.

Thus, true teams, in contrast to working groups, involve:

1. A small group.

   Teams can range in size from two to fifteen or so. Once a group gets too large it becomes very difficult for it to be anything more than a "working group," since the larger the group, the more difficult it becomes for the people to interact constructively. For this reason it is better for large groups to break into sub-teams rather than try to function as a single team.

   Ten people are far more likely than fifty to live in committed, loving community with each other, to work through their differences toward a common vision and to hold themselves accountable for the results.

   Large groups face many disadvantages:

   - Logistical difficulties such as finding enough space and time to get together.
   - More complex constraints, such as crowd or herd behaviors,

that prevent the intense and authentic sharing of lives and views that are necessary to build a team. Consequently, large groups tend to have broader and more superficial statements of purpose that are usually established by the top leaders.
- Usually function according to more formal hierarchy, structure, policies and procedures due to the difficulty of maintaining the flexibility and spontaneity possible for small teams.
- Increased difficulty in selecting the right people for the right fit.
- Increased likelihood of frequent membership change with the accompanying destabilizing and demoralizing potentials.
- Harder to find roles and tasks for each member that match their gifts and skills.
- Problematic communication among so many:
  - Harder to accomplish so more likely neglected.
  - Greater chance of misinterpretation.
- Difficult to develop and maintain personal relationships – in a team of 15 people there are 105 pairs of one-on-one relationships![1]
- Increased potential for conflict.
- Harder to develop members' callings, gifts and skills.
- Less feasible for everyone to contribute to the team.

On the other hand, if the group is too small, it may suffer from the following problems:

- Insufficient resources.
- Limited gifts and skills.
- Lack of creativity.
- Poor problem solving.

---

[1] Here is the formula: the number of people in the group times that number minus one, divided by two equals the total number of potential relationships. Thus, a group of 2 people has 1 relational bond (2 x 1 ÷ 2 = 1), a group of 10 people contains 45 relationships (10 x 9 ÷ 2 = 45), and a group of 15 people potentially contains 105 distinct relationships (15 x 14 ÷ 2 = 105).

While the exact size of an appropriate team will vary according to the situation, generally speaking the team should be kept as small as possible while maintaining the ability to function effectively.

2. Loving community.

    The Godhead functions as a team, but the Father, Son and Holy Spirit *first* fellowship together – that is their essential nature.

    When God created man and woman, His desire was that they *first* love one another before they did anything together.

    When Jesus built His team, His first priority for them was that they be "with Him."

    He appointed twelve – designating them apostles – that they might be with Him and that He might send them out to preach and to have authority to drive out demons. (Mark 3:15-15)

    The church, likewise, is primarily a living community of fellowship and love, rather than a task-driven, performance-oriented machine.

    The relational elements of team-life must not be sacrificed for the tasks the team must accomplish. Teams in which the members love one another, spend time together as friends and care for one another will be powerful.

3. Commitment to each other.

    Out of relational community will come the team members' recognition of and respect for one another's giftings and callings. Along with this recognition and respect will also come each member's personal commitment to the other team members – to do all he can to help them be all they can be in Christ.

> *Now that I, your Lord and Teacher, have washed your feet, you also should wash one another's feet. (John 13:14)*

Teams that are committed to each other will also enjoy a better corporate sense of humor and have more fun.

This genuine commitment cannot be planned or forced into existence. It grows from each team member genuinely recognizing the bonds of the Holy Spirit that unite them. God has already united the members of the Christian team, but we must strive to *maintain* that unity:

> *Make every effort to keep the unity of the Spirit through the bond of peace. (Eph. 4:3)*

4. Complementary gifts and skills.

To be truly effective, teams must possess the right mix of gifts and skills. The right mix does not mean conformity – far from it! The right mix means differences.

A strong leadership team in a local church, for example, might have a diversity of:

a. Ministry gift orientations (Eph. 4:11). A team that consists only of evangelists will probably over-emphasize evangelism. A team that consists only of teachers will probably under-emphasize evangelism and/or pastoral concerns. By contrast, a team that has a relative balance of ministry gift orientations will be more balanced in its vision and approach.[2]

---

[2] It is highly unlikely that *all* of the ministry offices of Ephesians 4:11 would be present in one local church. It is, however, not only possible but highly desirable to have all the ministry gift *orientations* present in a single leadership team.

b. Interpersonal skills. Without some "people" people on the team it is likely to become too task-oriented and lose its relational warmth. Moreover, a healthy team needs certain members with strong abilities in the areas of communication, conflict management, motivation and persuasion.
c. Strategic abilities. Every team needs a "big picture" visionary along with those who have planning, problem-solving and decision-making skills.
d. Technical expertise. The leadership team of a local church will probably need people who are qualified in the areas of finances, management, administration, construction and maintenance, as well as those skilled in teaching and counseling, etc. A variety of areas of technical expertise brings a diversity of perspectives as well as abilities that is a great strength to a team.

We must avoid three common errors:

a. Forming teams on the basis of similarity of gift or calling. So many leaders form teams around themselves consisting of people who are just like they are. This is the worst thing a leader can do. The wise leader will surround himself with people whose strengths make up for his own weaknesses.
b. Forming teams on the basis of personal compatibility. We must not build teams that consist only of people we personally like or of people whose personalities are similar to our own. God will use personality conflicts to change and mature us all. Moreover we must have the variety of perspectives that only a diversity of personalities can bring. Forming a team on the basis of personal compatibility will make life much easier but it will also be considerably less effective.

c. Forming teams on the basis of formal position in the organization. The primary basis for participation in a team must be calling, gifting and skills, not mere formality. People should not be invited to participate in a leadership team merely because it is "polite" to do so or merely because they would be "offended" if not invited.

5. Common vision, goals and working approach.

For a team to be effective, its members must genuinely share long-term vision as well as short-term goals. Moreover, both vision and goals must be based on the solid conviction that they genuinely represent the will of God for the organization. Then the team must move ahead with a common working approach.

First, teams must develop a common vision. The blessing of God abides upon a team that functions in unity (Ps. 133). Heart unity is only possible when the team members genuinely share the same vision. It is not sufficient for members to possess strong visions for their own individual ministries; they must first be committed to a common *team*-vision. When team members are more committed to the advancement of their own personal agendas than they are to the shared team-vision, they undermine the team's power.

Without a shared vision there is no foundation, motivation, direction or focus for the team. It is simply a working group of individuals whose energies are all directed towards their individual roles and responsibilities. But with a common vision there are many benefits:

a. A common vision builds strength.

Without a clear vision people are weak. They meander in life, wandering from this to that, with no passion, no motivation, no conviction and no strength. However, when there is a strong and clear vision in a team, the members are disciplined and focused. They work together with energy and unity.

I appeal to you, brothers, in the name of our Lord Jesus Christ, that all of you agree with one another so that there may be no divisions among you and that you may be perfectly united in mind and thought. (1 Cor. 1:10)

Paul is not only writing about unity of doctrine in 1 Corinthians 1:10, but his meaning embraces unity of vision. When we have a common vision, we will enjoy harmony, peace, oneness of mind and high levels of responsibility, commitment and morale.

b. A common vision reduces frustration.

There are both negative and positive sides to vision. Our long-term vision tells us not only what we should do, but also what we should not do.[3] Therefore, we can focus on and accomplish what we are called to do, leaving the rest to whomever is called to do it and avoiding the frustration and burnout that inevitably accompany the attempt to "do it all."

c. A common vision generates cooperation.

True teams possess cooperation and integration so that all the various aspects and facets work together instead of competing against each other as separate, isolated identities with completely different, often conflicting, agendas.

---

[3] Jesus is our perfect example here. He did not merely do "good things," but He focused on doing only what He knew was His Father's will. Many times this meant ignoring opportunities for ministry (e.g., Mark 1:36-39) but Jesus did so without guilt because He was committed to doing *only* what was His Father's will (John 8:29).

d. A common vision creates concentration.

The light of the sun will warm the surface of a dry leaf that is on the ground. But if you focus that light through a magnifying glass you will set the leaf on fire. Moreover, if you concentrate light even more by using a laser beam, you will be able to cut through a block of steel. As we focus our energies – individually and as a church – we will have considerably more energy and a greater impact.

Paul and Jesus were both focused on the purposes of God:

Brothers, I do not consider myself yet to have taken hold of it. But one thing I do: Forgetting what is behind and straining toward what is ahead, I press on toward the goal to win the prize for which God has called me heavenward in Christ Jesus. (Phil. 3:13-14)

I offered my back to those who beat me, my cheeks to those who pulled out my beard; I did not hide my face from mocking and spitting. Because the Sovereign LORD *helps me, I will not be disgraced. Therefore have I set my face like flint, and I know I will not be put to shame. (Is. 50:6-7)*

The more we allow our energies to be diffused, the less success we will have in fulfilling God's will. It is better to be excellent at a few things than mediocre at many. Thus a common vision creates concentration.

e. A common vision helps resolve conflict.

The shared vision becomes a meaningful standard against which to resolve clashes between the interests of the individual and the interests of the team. Armed with team purpose, everyone on the team knows when an individual may be getting out of line and then must put the team first or risk breaking it apart.

f. A common vision assists evaluation.

How do we evaluate our lives and our ministries? We certainly do not do it by comparing ourselves with others. We should evaluate our lives by asking:

- What has God called us to do? What is our vision?
- How well are we accomplishing our vision?

Honest evaluation is only possible when we have first established a clear vision.

Second, teams must develop common goals. Specific goals provide clear and tangible footholds for several reasons:

g. A journey of a thousand miles begins with a single step. Or, to put it another way, how do you eat an elephant? One bite at a time, of course! Teams who try to accomplish the extraordinary must learn the discipline of breaking down big problems and opportunities into small, doable steps. Problems and opportunities that are conceived of too broadly overwhelm us, but anybody can take "just one more step." Thus, when the journey is broken down into achievable goals and milestones, the task is more easily understood and accomplished.

For example, a church movement may have a long-term vision to plant new churches within 20 unreached people groups. An appropriate goal for this year might be to plant new churches in one of them. The long-term vision is 20; the short-term goal is one. This makes the vision achievable – step-by-step.

h. With clear goals, team prayer and discussions can focus on how to achieve them or whether to change them. In our example above, as things progress during the first year, the leadership team may realize that their vision is overly ambitious or perhaps not ambitious enough. They may realize they lack the necessary resources or training. In striving to achieve the short-term goal, the path to the fulfillment of the long-term vision becomes much clearer.

i. The attainability of specific goals helps teams maintain their focus on getting results. Without goals, the long-vision will typically be too big and broad for team members to maintain focus. Moreover, feeling themselves getting nowhere – as measured against the big vision – inevitably has a discouraging effect on teams.

j. Specific objectives have a leveling effect that is conducive to team behavior. When a small group of people accept a challenge to accomplish something great, their respective title, status or personality fades into the background. The only thing that matters is the team-goal with each individual striving to contribute towards that end.

k. Specific goals allow the team to achieve small wins as it pursues its long-term vision. Small wins are invaluable to building team members' commitment and overcoming the inevitable obstacles that stand in the team's way. Small wins enable teams to build momentum and to create a climate in which success is not only seen as possible, but imminent.

There is nothing more discouraging than starting off with a failure, so wise teams include a few early successes in their plan.

1. Team goals are compelling.

   They challenge the people on the team to commit themselves, as a team, to make a difference. The excitement and urgency of the goal drive the team forward. Impossible for individuals to achieve but attainable by the team, it becomes their special challenge.

Third, teams also need to develop a common approach – how they will work together to accomplish their purpose. In fact, they should invest as much time and effort crafting their working approach as shaping their purpose. Team members must agree on:

- How particular responsibilities will be assumed.
- How schedules will be set and adhered to.
- The skills that need to be developed.
- How resources will be obtained and used.
- How the team will make and modify decisions (including when and how to modify the working approach itself).
- How team members will support each other.
- How team members will be accountable to each other.

Naturally, the complete working approach of a team will evolve over time. It is a mistake for people to think they must assemble a team at the beginning with "everything in perfect place." Nevertheless, the more a team wrestles with the above issues of approach, the more effectively it will proceed and the better equipped it will be to handle the inevitable conflicts that arise.

6. Mutual accountability.

   ... Yes, all of you be submissive to one another, and be clothed with humility, for "God resists the proud, but gives grace to the humble." (1 Pet. 5:5, NKJV)

Being part of a leadership team means being mutually accountable. Traditionally, people know they should be accountable to the leader. But in a team, people must be accountable to each other. Furthermore, this includes every member of the team, including the leader himself.

At its core, accountability is about two vital aspects of a team: commitment and trust. As each member promises to hold himself accountable to the team's vision, goals and working approach, each one earns the right to express his own views about all aspects of what the team is and does, and to have his views receive a fair and constructive hearing. Then by acting in a truly accountable way and thus following through on his promise, each team member preserves and strengthens the trust upon which the team must be built.

Many people are naturally cautious about committing themselves to others. Thus, mutual promises and accountability cannot be coerced any more than people can be forced to trust one another. However, the process of development of the team's vision, goals and approach will often have the effect of increasing the mutual commitment of team members to each other. Accountability tends to naturally grow in a team that has invested significant time and energy in determining what it is to do and how it is to do it.

Thus, people who are truly committed and accountable to team results are the ones who develop both a strong team purpose and an agreed-upon approach. Alternatively, groups that lack mutual accountability have not shaped a common vision and approach that can sustain them as a team.

From all the above, it is evident that genuine teams are not easy to build or maintain. There is a high cost involved in teams, but it will be highly rewarding.

Please complete the following evaluation before you continue.

EVALUATION

Healthy teams do not spring up by themselves. It is hard work to build an effective team. To assist you in your own team development we have included this guide to evaluation.

Please think about each of the six basic elements of teams as you assess your team's current situation:

1. Are you small enough in number?

    a. Can you get together easily and quickly?
    b. Can you communicate with all team members easily and frequently?
    c. Do all members interact openly and honestly in your discussions?
    d. Does each member understand the others' callings, giftings, skills and roles?
    e. Do you need more people on the team to achieve your purposes?
    f. If you're too big, is it possible or necessary to break into sub-teams?

2. Do you live and function in loving community?

    a. Do team members genuinely care for each other or are you just politely "putting up" with one another?
    b. Is this care genuine – that is, is it reflected in specific actions of love?
    c. Do you spend time together as friends, apart from "business" matters?
    d. Is there a sense that "if one of us fails, we all fail"?

3. Are you genuinely committed to each other's personal growth and success?

   a. Do you value each other as brethren in the Lord, each with a specific purpose for his or her life, or are you just "using" one another's gifts and skills to help yourself achieve your own purpose?
   b. Is mutual respect present between all members?
   c. Does each member clearly recognize the specific callings and purposes of the others?
   d. What concrete steps do you take to help one another grow?
   e. Is every team member willing to help the others grow and fulfill God's purposes?
   f. Do you often laugh and have fun together?

4. Does your team possess the right mix of gifts and skills?

   a. Does your team have a relative balance of the ministry gifts (Eph. 4) and the gifts of the Spirit (1 Cor. 12), or is it lopsided?
   b. Are there any critical gifts or skills that are obviously lacking?
   c. Do you have some "people" people on the team or are you all task-oriented?
   d. Is there a strong "visionary" as well as those with planning, problem-solving and decision-making skills?
   e. What are the necessary areas of technical expertise your team needs and are they adequately represented?
   f. What is the personality mix like in your team; is there sufficient diversity?
   g. Is the team obligated to have certain "token" members or do all members function and participate seriously?

5. Do you share a common vision, common goals and a clear working approach?

    a. Is your vision truly a *team*-vision or is it just one individual's vision (e.g., the leader's)?
    b. Is your vision clear? Do all team members understand it and can they articulate it without relying on ambiguous abstractions?
    c. Do members defend the vision, refer to it frequently and actively explore its implications?
    d. Are members excited by the vision?
    e. Are your goals truly the team's goals or are they just one individual's goals (e.g., the leader's)?
    f. Are your goals clear, simple and somehow measurable?
    g. Are your goals realistic as well as ambitious? Do they provide for small wins along the way?
    h. Do all members agree on the team goals and their relative importance?
    i. Is your working approach concrete, clear and understood and agreed to by everyone? Will it result in the achievement of the objectives?
    j. Does your working approach use and enhance the gifts and skills of all members?
    k. Does it provide for its own modification and improvement over time?

6. Do you have a healthy sense of mutual accountability in your team?

    a. Are you individually and jointly accountable for the team's vision, goals and working approach?
    b. Can you and do you measure progress against specific goals?
    c. Do all members feel responsible for all goals?
    d. Are the members clear on what they are individually responsible for and jointly responsible for?

Answering these questions can establish the degree of health your team enjoys – indeed, it can establish whether or not your group is even a real "team" in the first place. Your answers will also show you where and how to strengthen your team. These questions set a very high standard (they do reflect a relative "dream team") and answering them honestly may reveal a harder challenge than you expected. However, facing reality will be a giant step taken toward achieving the full potential of your team.

chapter 4

The Benefits of Teams

When teams are healthy, they – more than the individual – become the critical building blocks of the entire organization.

Here are some of the many benefits of teams:

1. Teams bring together complementary callings, gifts, skills and experiences that, by definition, *exceed* those of any one member of the team.

   There is an old saying, "Two heads are better than one." Or, as one man put it, "None of us is as smart as all of us." None of us is as strong, or as gifted, or as skilled, or as experienced as all of us.

   > **TEAM**
   > **T**ogether **E**veryone **A**chieves **M**ore!

   Every believer has a distinct calling from God as well as unique gifts, talents, strengths, experiences and abilities. Every believer also has individual viewpoints, concerns and sensitivities. When we join together in a team, we are able to share all these things with each other in our pursuit of a common vision.

2. *Focus*. In a team each member is released to focus on what he does best while the whole team accomplishes the whole task. This means the members will enjoy their tasks more and will do them better. Additionally, they will not "burn out" as easily.

3. *Community*. Teams provide a dimension of community in which the members grow in relationship, trust and accountability together. In healthy teams, the members reinforce each other's intentions to pursue the team purpose above and beyond what is possible for any individual working by himself. Moreover they are committed to mutual support and care for one another.

4. Teams are more *flexible and creative* than individuals who are caught in a rut of organizational bureaucracies able only to function according to their narrow task definitions.

5. Healthy teams *communicate* openly in a way that supports the improvement of decision-making, problem solving and the taking of new initiatives.

6. Because of their collective commitment, teams are often more open to *change* than individuals who have to fend for themselves.

7. Teams help develop a *shared sense of direction* throughout the organization. By having a number of people actively "promote" the team's vision, those throughout the whole organization will more readily accept and cooperate with the vision than if it were promoted merely by one individual leader.

8. Because of the broader ownership of the vision and the process, teams create increased *commitment* and *morale* – not only among team members, but throughout the organization.

9. Teams *enjoy* their work more. This is no trivial matter since the more we enjoy what we're doing, the better we'll do it. This

enjoyment comes from the times of celebration that a healthy team has, as well as, most importantly, from the deep satisfaction of having been a part of something larger than oneself.

The world is going through a time of rapid and extensive change. To stay relevant and effective the church must change too.[4] The complex nature of Christian ministry in the 21st century practically requires leaders to work in teams. Many times, teams offer the best means of responding to the challenges that the church faces. We need effective leadership teams to lead the church into effective ministry in the new century. One person, even an incredibly gifted and talented leader, is unlikely to be strong enough, gifted enough or wise enough to bring the necessary change to the whole church.

The following table shows a number of ways that a team leadership structure differs from a traditional leadership structure.

Traditional Leadership Versus Team Leadership	
Traditional Leadership Structure	**Team Leadership Structure**
Hierarchical structure of leadership and power	More sharing of leadership and power within the team
Each co-worker is responsible for only a portion of the vision; they may not realize how all the parts fit together into a whole	Team members work together to lead the whole organization
Co-workers are all focused on their own individual agendas	Team members focus on the team's vision and goals

---

[4] While maintaining the eternal and unchanging truths of the Word of God, of course.

Co-workers may develop a competitive attitude toward other co-workers	Co-workers are allied together, sharing a common vision, even though they may represent different areas of the organization
Co-workers attend occasional meetings where information is told to them	Team members must meet frequently to set goals, resolve problems and review progress
Success depends on individuals performing well	Success depends on the team

We are not suggesting that teams are the only proper context for leaders to function in at all times. In fact, the best kind of organizational leadership is often found in a balance between individual and team efforts – rather than in replacing one with the other.

chapter 5

The Characteristics of a Healthy Team

When a team is healthy and functions well, it is like a symphony orchestra that has dozens of individuals playing many different instruments but doing so in perfect harmony. The audience listening to such an orchestra can appreciate the fruits of their unity. But an excellent concert performance never just happens by itself. An incredible amount of work goes into bringing all the musicians into unity:

- The conductor must decide which pieces of music to play and in what order.
- The talents of each member must be accurately determined.
- Each member must make himself and his talents sufficiently available to the whole orchestra.
- The conductor must use each musician to the fullest extent of his ability.
- Rules of music must be observed.
- Many hours of practicing together according to the established rules must occur.
- All the necessary musicians and instruments must be present.
- The conductor must be capable of building and maintaining the team.

Only with all these things in place can a group of musicians become an excellent orchestra.

In the same way, an effective Christian leadership team must work very hard:

- It must determine its vision and goals.
- The members of the team must know each other's callings, giftings and skills.
- Each person must submit himself to the overall purpose of the whole team.
- Each person must be mobilized to the fullest extent of his calling and capacity.
- The working approach of the team must be determined.
- Team meetings must be relevant and effective.
- The team must possess the appropriate divine, human and material resources.
- The team leader must be effective.

Only with all these things in place can a group of Christian co-workers become an effective leadership team.

Characteristics of a Healthy Team

A healthy team has godly, committed, gifted and competent members who use open communication in an environment of prayer where issues get solved by consensus before the Lord as the team pursues a shared vision.

Thus, the team itself is characterized by:

- **Environment of prayer.**

    The first disciples spent time together in prayer – especially when faced with crises or decisions.

    After Jesus had left, but before the Holy Spirit fell:

    > *They all joined together constantly in prayer, along with the women and Mary the mother of Jesus, and with His brothers. (Acts 1:14)*

During the first days after Pentecost when the church was experiencing supernatural power and very rapid growth:

> *They devoted themselves to the apostles' teaching and to the fellowship, to the breaking of bread and to prayer. (Acts 2:42)*

When Peter was imprisoned:

> *So Peter was kept in prison, but the church was earnestly praying to God for him. (Acts 12:5)*

The ultimate leader of the team is the Lord Jesus. Therefore, His presence, wisdom and direction must be sought continually by the team.

- **A shared vision.**

In a healthy team, the members share a common vision and common goals that proceed from that vision, and they work collaboratively to achieve their purpose.

Moreover, the vision and the goals must reflect the will of God. When the co-workers deeply believe that God is behind the team, they will work at their highest capacity.

Because of the magnitude of the task, the team members realize their need for one another. Since it draws together people with a diversity of callings, backgrounds and experiences, the whole team possesses a base of wisdom and knowledge that no single individual could possess.

- **Frequent and meaningful communication.**

The team members communicate frequently and openly with each other. They discuss issues and when problems arise, they resolve them together.

Effective teams spend about 60-70% of their communication time talking about vision, goals and tasks. In teams that communicate well, 15-20% of all statements show support or encouragement. The remainder of the communication time (about 10-15% of the total) includes statements of disagreement as well as discussion of topics unrelated to the task. If the proportion of different kinds of communication varies greatly from these averages, a team's success plummets.[5]

Thus, a healthy team's communication will reflect these priorities:

1. Vision, goals and tasks.
2. Mutual support and encouragement.
3. Disagreements and unrelated topics.

- **Inclusive attitude.**

People who work well in teams acknowledge the contributions that the other members have made to their lives and to the success of the team. Healthy teams will be marked by a noncompetitive atmosphere. When there is no jealousy then the people will share their ideas freely and will work with one another, unconcerned that a co-worker will "steal the credit" for a victory.

> *Love is patient, love is kind. It does not envy, it does not boast, it is not proud. (1 Cor. 13:4)*

> *For I am afraid that when I come I may not find you as I want you to be, and you may not find me as you want me to be. I fear that there may be quarreling, jealousy, outbursts of anger, factions, slander, gossip, arrogance and disorder. (2 Cor. 12:20)*

---

[5] Susan A. Wheelan. (1999). *Creating Effective Teams: A Guide for Members and Leaders.* Thousand Oaks, CA: Sage Publications, p. 58.

> *The acts of the sinful nature are obvious: sexual immorality, impurity and debauchery; idolatry and witchcraft; hatred, discord, jealousy, fits of rage, selfish ambition, dissensions, factions and envy; drunkenness, orgies, and the like. I warn you, as I did before, that those who live like this will not inherit the Kingdom of God. (Gal. 5:19-21)*

> *It is true that some preach Christ out of envy and rivalry ... (Phil. 1:15)*

> *At one time we too were foolish, disobedient, deceived and enslaved by all kinds of passions and pleasures. We lived in malice and envy, being hated and hating one another. But when the kindness and love of God our Savior appeared, He saved us ... I want you to stress these things, so that those who have trusted in God may be careful to devote themselves to doing what is good ... (Tit. 3:3-8)*

> *But if you harbor bitter envy and selfish ambition in your hearts, do not boast about it or deny the truth. Such "wisdom" does not come down from heaven but is earthly, unspiritual, of the devil. For where you have envy and selfish ambition, there you find disorder and every evil practice. (Jam. 3:14-16)*

> *Therefore, rid yourselves of all malice and all deceit, hypocrisy, envy, and slander of every kind. (1 Pet. 2:1)*

- **Shared responsibility.**

A healthy team will have one overall leader, but the whole team will bear responsibility for the ultimate outcome of its collective efforts. Consequently, members of a healthy team will think of the good of the team and of the whole church or ministry before themselves.

- **Not threatened by differences.**

  As the team members all share their input, there are bound to be frequent differences. Differences themselves are not bad; it is what we do with them that matters. Healthy teams view differences of opinion as opportunities to test and refine their work. They listen well and critique issues without attacking people. If the members of the team were all the same, then they would never have the opportunity to explore alternative approaches or engage in healthy differences of opinion. Consequently, healthy teams value their diversity of ministry gift orientations, callings, giftings, skills, experiences and personalities.

- **Decision-making by consensus.**

  This does not mean that everyone must decide every issue that ever comes up. Many – perhaps most – decisions should be left to individual co-workers to make as they see fit according to their own areas of responsibility.

  This also does not mean that everyone must eventually agree before any action is ever taken. Sometimes an action must be taken before agreement is reached – either to solve a problem or advance with an opportunity. It is, however, important that a general consensus is reached on major issues – that is, every member, in spite of his personal disagreement, is willing to go ahead and support the decision. A consensus occurs when all team members agree that a particular action is acceptable, even though it is not necessarily the first choice of every member.

  A leadership team that corporately addresses every issue that comes up and that always waits for a 100% agreement before ever advancing with any decision will not accomplish much!

Thus, an effective team leader must find a balance between independent, decisive thinking on one hand and collecting and evaluating ideas and working toward a team consensus on the other. The issue is not so much whether a leader should make individual or consensus decisions. Of more practical importance for effective leadership is recognizing which style of decision-making is necessary for each situation.

Decisions that are best made by the team leader or by another team member without necessarily getting team members' input include minor and political issues, crises, and strategic decisions where the group members don't see or understand the big picture.

Here are some general principles that will help:

- ~ When commitment to implementing the decision is important, it is best to achieving consensus with the team members before making the final decision.
- ~ When creativity is important for solving a major problem, it is best to involve a group of people from different specialties – including people outside the team if necessary. The various points of view are likely to generate creative thinking. Just listening to the various view points might spark everyone's thinking for arriving at a useful decision.
- ~ In general, important decisions are better suited for group decision-making than minor decisions. It is, however, sometimes difficult to gauge how important a decision might be to individual team members.
- ~ When a strategic decision is needed and most team members do not understand the big picture, independent decision-making from the leader might be best. A good plan may be to collect a few points of view from several on the team in a consultative style without implying that you are searching for consensus.

- When an issue is so political that it is difficult to obtain an unbiased point of view from team members, it is probably best for the leader to make the decision independently.
- When time is at a premium, such as in a crisis, unilateral decision-making is usually best. If it appears that input from others is needed, then it might be wise to use participative decision-making but do it within a tight time limit such as a two-hour meeting.

Thus, an effective team leader must find a balance between independent decision-making on one hand and building a team consensus on the other. It all depends on the situation.

- **Clear role assignments that match team members' callings, giftings and talents.**

For the team to succeed, team members need clear-cut division of roles. Healthy teams have individuals who can define roles for themselves and work with the roles that the other team members have developed.

- **Team members are genuinely interested in and concerned for one another.**

As we have already seen, teams in which the members love one another, spend time together as friends and care for one another will be powerful. Such teams will not be marked by competitiveness but by trust, cooperation and servanthood.

Moreover, the personal commitment of the co-workers to one another will ensure that they work through conflict successfully.

- **Recognize that conflict is a healthy and necessary part of team interaction.**

Since teams are made up of imperfect human beings, conflict is a common part of team life – as the experience of the Early Church shows. In fact, the absence of conflict can be quite detrimental to a team. We will discuss conflict later.

- **Positive attitude.**

Healthy teams don't squash innovation by constantly criticizing new ideas. Instead they welcome new ideas from both within and without their own ranks and respond positively to the suggestions and requests from their own members and from others.

In addition, when difficulties arise, co-workers should look for solutions instead of just complaining about the problems. Team members should always look for the good in each other and believe the best about the team.

> [Love] always protects, always trusts, always hopes, always perseveres. (1 Cor. 13:7)

- **Continual learning.**

One's own refusal to change will not stop the fact that the world is changing rapidly; it will only hinder one's own ability to reach the world with the Gospel. Every day brings new challenges and new opportunities. Consequently, a healthy leadership team must be committed to continuous, lifelong learning and will seek opportunities to develop in all areas of gifting and ability. We will never get to the point where we know it all (or even the point where we know "enough") and can stop learning.

In addition, God has called His Church to be continually growing and maturing; and growth involves change – always!

Instead, speaking the truth in love, we will in all things grow up into Him who is the Head, that is, Christ. (Eph. 4:15)

Characteristics of a Healthy Team Member

Healthy teams are made up of healthy people. If the members of the team are personally dysfunctional, that will be reflected in the life of the team – and, in turn, will be reflected in the life of the entire church or ministry.

Let's revisit our definition of a healthy team: a healthy team has godly, committed, gifted and competent members who use open communication in an environment of prayer where issues get solved by consensus before the Lord as the team pursues a shared vision.

Thus, a healthy team member is characterized by:

- **Personal commitment to God.**

  The personal commitment to God in the heart of every member will cause each member to give his absolute best effort to the team's activities. Commitment to God lies at the heart of our commitment to one another. Our passion for the team is the test and indicator of our passion for God. If we are not truly committed to one another, then we are not truly committed to God.

- **Personal godliness of character.**

  An otherwise healthy team will be undermined and eventually destroyed by the unchecked presence of sin in the lives of its members. Godly co-workers establish godly teams that lead godly churches and ministries. In addition to personal purity and holiness, other character requirements are honesty, reliability and cooperativeness.

- **Security in Christ.**

    A healthy team member is not trying to "be someone." Consequently, he is not personally threatened by disagreement or diversity. He has no personal agenda so he is genuinely committed to the shared vision. Additionally, he will not always be calling attention to himself and his own accomplishments since he is not driven by the need to be recognized. Instead he will be able to give compliments, credit and recognition to other team members.

- **Clear understanding of his own calling.**

    Therefore knows where he fits – and where he doesn't belong, too.

- **Possesses the necessary skills and capabilities to fulfill his own responsibilities in the team.**

- **Flexibility.**

    Healthy team members are willing to listen to new ideas and to try new methods. Furthermore, each member must be capable of seeing things from the perspectives of the others on the team and not only from his own perspective.

- **Humility.**

    Each co-worker should recognize that all the members of the team must work together to fulfill God's purposes. This means each member is dependent on the others to solve the hardest problems and to win the greatest victories. Credit for success should always be shared by the whole team. Co-workers should use words like *we*, *us* and *our*, instead of *I*, *me* and *mine* – especially when discussing team achievements.

- **Puts the vision of the team before his own vision.**

This is the key difference between working groups of individuals and genuine teams. This is the key issue of synergy.

- **Respects appropriate personal boundaries.**

Good team members do not ask prying questions about the issues of other members. While committed to genuine openness and accountability, they realize that team unity does not necessarily require knowledge of every personal detail of every team member's life. Moreover, they will certainly not be guilty of gossip.

> *A gossip betrays a confidence, but a trustworthy man keeps a secret. (Prov. 11:13)*

> *Make it your ambition to lead a quiet life, to mind your own business and to work with your hands, just as we told you, (1 Thess. 4:11)*

> *We hear that some among you are idle. They are not busy; they are busybodies. (2 Thess. 3:11)*

> *But let none of you suffer as a murderer, a thief, an evildoer, or as a busybody in other people's matters. (1 Pet. 4:15, NKJV)*

- **Admits when he's wrong.**

Team members should accept personal responsibility when necessary by admitting their mistakes and apologizing.

> *Therefore confess your sins to each other and pray for each other so that you may be healed … (Jam. 5:16)*

The admission of errors builds trust in the team. Moreover it keeps each member pure before God.

- **Is a good listener.**

   My dear brothers, take note of this: Everyone should be quick to listen, slow to speak ... (Jam. 1:19)

   It comes naturally to most of us to speak more than we listen. However, you demonstrate respect and caring by listening carefully to others and summarizing what they have said to clarify your understanding (a process called "active listening"). When a person feels you are genuinely trying to understand his point of view, it builds trust.

- **Is courteous and respectful.**

   Healthy teams thrive on respectful treatment of each member. We should not demand or command, but use words like "please" and "thank you."

   Finally, all of you be of one mind, having compassion for one another; love as brothers, be tenderhearted, be courteous; (1 Pet. 3:8, NKJV)

- **Gives positive and negative feedback in a positive way.**

   Regarding positive feedback, team members should express thanks and gratitude *for* one another *to* one another. Paul did this:

   First, I thank my God through Jesus Christ for all of you, because your faith is being reported all over the world. (Rom. 1:8)

   I thank my God every time I remember you. (Phil. 1:3)

> *We ought always to thank God for you, brothers, and rightly so, because your faith is growing more and more, and the love every one of you has for each other is increasing. Therefore, among God's churches we boast about your perseverance and faith in all the persecutions and trials you are enduring. (2 Thess. 1:3-4)*

People need the encouragement that this will give them. Sometimes we are so afraid of someone becoming puffed up with pride that we neglect to share sufficient affirmation with them. Our team members need encouragement as they persist in their journey to fulfill the vision, and they need it frequently. Moreover, this will also build the team's confidence. Team members' belief in each other creates a self-fulfilling prophecy: people act in ways that are consistent with others' expectations of them. Team members who truly believe in each other and who express that confidence through high expectations will bring out the very best in the team as a whole.

Regarding negative feedback, Paul set us an excellent example of how to do this. Notice how he affirmed both the Corinthians and the Colossians before bringing serious correction to them:

> *I always thank God for you because of His grace given you in Christ Jesus. For in Him you have been enriched in every way – in all your speaking and in all your knowledge – because our testimony about Christ was confirmed in you. Therefore you do not lack any spiritual gift as you eagerly wait for our Lord Jesus Christ to be revealed. He will keep you strong to the end, so that you will be blameless on the day of our Lord Jesus Christ. (1 Cor. 1:4-8)*

> *How can we thank God enough for you in return for all the joy we have in the presence of our God because of you? (1 Thess. 3:9)*

We always thank God, the Father of our Lord Jesus Christ, when we pray for you, because we have heard of your faith in Christ Jesus and of the love you have for all the saints – the faith and love that spring from the hope that is stored up for you in heaven and that you have already heard about in the Word of Truth, the Gospel that has come to you. All over the world this Gospel is bearing fruit and growing, just as it has been doing among you since the day you heard it and understood God's grace in all its truth. You learned it from Epaphras, our dear fellow servant, who is a faithful minister of Christ on our behalf, and who also told us of your love in the Spirit. (Col. 1:3-8)

Paul's entire reason for writing to both the Corinthians and Colossians was to rebuke them, and he started both letters with affirmations! And after correcting the Corinthians look how he spoke to them:

I do not say this to condemn you; I have said before that you have such a place in our hearts that we would live or die with you. I have great confidence in you; I take great pride in you. I am greatly encouraged; in all our troubles my joy knows no bounds ... I am glad I can have complete confidence in you. (2 Cor. 7:3-4, 16)

This is Paul's example to us of how to bring correction: start with affirmation and finish with affirmation. The following is a summary of how to share negative feedback with others:

~ It should start with affirmation (e.g., 1 Cor. 1:4-8). This is godlier and it will also increase the likelihood of the person responding favorably because they know that the feedback is given for their benefit and from a heart of love.
~ To be effective, affirmation should be specific. Paul didn't tell the Colossians something vague like, "You're

doing great!" He was specific: "We've heard of your faith and love ..."

- ~ It should be private. Except in the case of extreme error or sin (e.g., 1 Tim. 5:20), you should never correct someone in front of another.
- ~ It should be constructive. Never give someone feedback that is not intended to help the individual become a more effective Christian or leader. For example, telling someone they are too old to build an effective relationship with younger believers is not constructive because age is something that cannot be changed.
- ~ It should be specific without being accusatory. Vague criticism will only minister condemnation and discouragement. Specific feedback will assist the person to improve their behavior.
- ~ It should be given as soon as possible after the incident occurred. Letting it go for too long will only reduce the effectiveness of your feedback as well as make the person feel a little betrayed: "If I really was wrong, why did you wait so long to tell me?"
- ~ Speak only for yourself. Don't imply that everyone in the group feels the way you do (this is commonly done but rarely accurate), even if they do. Saying so will only make the person feel "ganged up on," causing them to become defensive and less likely to receive correction.
- ~ Avoid exaggerations. Statements like, "You always ..." are not likely to be true and will probably have the effect of reducing the credibility of everything you're saying.
- ~ It should finish with affirmation (e.g., 2 Cor. 7:3-4, 16).

- **Receives positive and negative feedback in a positive way.**

Of course, it is much easier to give feedback than to receive it – especially when it's negative! The following are some principles of how to receive correction:

- Don't interrupt them until they are finished.
- Restate the person's comments to make sure you understood.
- Resist the temptation to immediately justify yourself. For most of us, self-justification is the normal "knee-jerk" reaction to criticism of any kind.
- As the person is sharing, acknowledge valid points and ask questions to clarify the issue.
- Think carefully about what is said. It's better to reflect on the feedback than to respond hastily. This will not make you appear indecisive.
- As soon as practical, respond in the appropriate way. When a person asks you to change in some way, some possible responses include:
- "I'll do it. Thanks for the help."
- "I'm sorry. I can't do that, and here's why …"
- "I can do it under these circumstances …"
- "I need to think about it and get back to you."

Sometimes receiving positive feedback can be equally traumatic. A gracious response to compliments might be, "Thanks, I appreciate your saying that," or "Your opinion means a lot to me, so I'm glad you think so." Avoid making statements like, "Oh, it was nothing. I'm sure you could have done it better." Such self-deprecation not only has the appearance of false humility, it makes the person who complimented you sound foolish to have done so.

Characteristics of an Unhealthy Team Member

Co-workers who aren't team players can ruin their team's effectiveness by destroying a team from the inside out. In fact, just one person can seriously interfere with a team's ability to fulfill its divine purpose. A non-team player engages in uncooperative or self-serving behavior such as:

- **Working on low-priority tasks instead of helping co-workers complete more pressing parts of a task with a rapidly closing deadline.**

- **Doing only the tasks specifically assigned to him.**

    Faced with new difficulties, rather than show initiative and offer to assist co-workers, a non-team player might say, "That's not my job!"

- **Making negative comments about co-workers or attacking the quality of others' suggestions.**

    Brothers, do not slander one another. Anyone who speaks against his brother or judges him speaks against the law and judges it. When you judge the law, you are not keeping it, but sitting in judgment on it. (Jam. 4:11)

- **Destroying the foundation for trust in the team by breaking confidences or by maligning co-workers to those outside the group.**

    A perverse man stirs up dissension, and a gossip separates close friends. (Prov. 16:28)

    He who covers over an offense promotes love, but whoever repeats the matter separates close friends. (Prov. 17:9)

    Without wood a fire goes out; without gossip a quarrel dies down. As charcoal to embers and as wood to fire, so is a quarrelsome man for kindling strife. (Prov. 26:20-21)

- **Responding "I'll do it myself" when a co-worker asks for your help on a task.**

    This independent spirit breaks the community and interdependence of the group. Perhaps you *could* do it better by yourself, but doing it with your brother will accomplish more than just the task at hand – it will also build the team!

- **Hoarding essential information or ideas in an attempt to gain an advantage over a co-worker or to "get someone back."**

    These are terrible abuses of power and privilege. A healthy team is characterized by openly sharing all knowledge and ideas with everyone as appropriate. All the knowledge of the team belongs to the team and should be, at all times, accessible to the whole team.

- **Playing political games in an attempt to show someone, "I've got more power than you."**

    In a healthy team, what specific power each team member has must always be used for the good of the whole team and not for the expression of personal agendas.

The Perils of Groupthink

"Groupthink" is a well-documented phenomenon that teams must vigilantly avoid. It occurs when a group of people strives to minimize conflict at the expense of critical analysis and evaluation. Groupthink happens when the members of a team try so hard to get along that they never disagree, which results in a stagnation of ideas.

Unfortunately, a team mired in groupthink rarely recognizes its problem. Some of the signs of the presence of groupthink are:

- **Team members unquestioningly agree with their leader.**

    This is a major characteristic of groupthink. Thus, whenever group members believe in the infallibility of the leader (although this will rarely be stated overtly), the team is on dangerous ground.

- **Intolerance is shown toward members who do not agree with the group, labeling them trouble-makers simply because their opinions differ.**

- **A strong sense of team invulnerability.**

  This can be an illusion created when team members do not realistically assess the obstacles ahead of them.

- **An unfavorable stereotyped view of outsiders.**

- **Critics, opponents and competitors are ridiculed and not given serious consideration.**

- **Due to the social pressure within the group, it is very difficult for team members to express disagreements or even doubts.**

  This helps to maintain the illusion of internal harmony.

- **Team members are discouraged from looking outside the group for ideas and information.**

- **Facts that are inconsistent with the preferred alternative are prevented from being seriously considered or are discounted through a process of rationalization.**

- **If ethical issues are involved in the decision, the team's illusion of moral superiority makes it easy to justify a course of action that would normally be considered unethical by the members.**

Some ways that a team can protect itself from groupthink include:

- **Ask someone from outside the team to sit in on one of your meetings.**

Often an outsider to the team can identify unproductive behavior more readily than team members or the team leader can.

- **Ask a group member to deliberately play the role of "intentional adversary."**

After the team has prepared its plan regarding a certain issue, the intentional adversary then examines its details, looking for weaknesses such as unbiblical or unethical thinking, faulty logic, doubtful inferences, questionable assumptions, overlooked information, biased forecasts and misinterpreted data. He then prepares a formal critique and presents it to the whole team. The team then considers whether their plan can be revised to deal with the criticisms in a satisfactory manner. If not, they may try to generate additional solutions or postpone the decision.

- **Assign a team member to point out the negative ramifications of any suggestion.**

- **Encourage critical, independent thinking.**

- **Evaluate the quality of every idea on its own merits instead of agreeing due to the status or credibility of the person making the suggestion.**

- **Cultivate an atmosphere in which co-workers are expected to disagree if they see a potential problem.**

- **Hold a second-chance meeting for momentous decisions.**

For controversial, important decisions, it is useful to hold another meeting after the group reaches a preliminary consensus. This "second-chance meeting" allows co-workers time to reconsider the evidence and express any lingering doubts before making a final decision.

Too little constructive disagreement lulls a team into deadly complacency. Teams must diligently guard against groupthink – particularly in cultures that place a high value on group unity and harmony.

Effective Communication

Teams cannot function without open communication. Honest communication can only exist in an atmosphere of genuine acceptance. There are two miscommunication extremes that render teams ineffective:

- Continuous disagreement in which nothing ever really gets resolved.
- Everyone being too "nice" to ever challenge each other's ideas.

For the team to be effective, co-workers must be free to verbally disagree with each other's ideas as well as contribute and support their own suggestions. For meaningful and productive team communication, co-workers need to deal with each other in a manner that is frank, respectful and receptive.

Communication must be frank:

- When necessary, share constructive criticism in private without using a condescending or demeaning tone.
- Disagree with ideas in a diplomatic way.
- Assign accountability so that each team member knows his exact responsibilities.

Communication must be respectful:

- Acknowledge the validity of a co-worker's feelings without necessarily agreeing. ("I can understand why you would feel that way.")
- Don't issue demands or commands. Instead, always request politely.

- Remember that Jesus loves your co-worker so much, He died for him. Moreover, Jesus told you to love him and serve him.

Communication must be receptive.

- Don't assume a defensive mode when a co-worker offers constructive criticism.
- Look for common ground. Can you agree with any part of what the other person is saying? Are they right about anything?
- Always listen before talking, and thoughtfully anticipate the consequences of your words and actions.

Evaluating Team Progress

To stay healthy, a team should review its own progress at frequent intervals by having its members check their performance against their objectives to identify areas in which they believe their teamwork needs improvement. This helps eliminate any problems that are starting to occur, as well as exposing the need for additional help.

Team evaluations also provide insight into opportunities for advancement that may have gone previously unnoticed.

Teams that are very busy will usually not want to pause for such reflection, but they need to. This is a critically important use of time. Although it seems like a waste of precious time, to take five minutes of a meeting to discuss how the team members are working together, and to spend an entire meeting every two months or so to discuss how the team is functioning, will save time and frustration in the long run.

Strategic Press
www.StrategicPress.org

Strategic Press is a division of Strategic Global Assistance, Inc.
www.sgai.org

513 S. Main St. Suite 2
Elkhart, IN 46516
U.S.A

+1-844-532-3371 (LEADER-1)

www.ingramcontent.com/pod-product-compliance
Lightning Source LLC
LaVergne TN
LVHW051711080426
835511LV00017B/2852